The Forgotten Rose

Mary Whalen

Monday Creek Publishing
Ohio USA

Copyright © 2019 Mary Whalen

All rights reserved.
ISBN-13: 978-0692066386

Dedication

Thank you to my sisters, Terri and Dee, for all your help and support.

*For where your treasure is,
there will your heart be also.*
Luke 12:34

A Bright Morning

Morning would find her pulling her hand-stitched crazy quilt up over her feather bed. Mary Hannah slipped on her shawl and stepped out on the back porch of her two-room cottage, ready to start the day. She followed the path to her garden where she pulled weeds and tended to her young plants. She loved the earthy smell of the dirt on her hands, moist from the morning dew.

Next, she walks to check on her favorite flower, a beautiful red rosebush that is climbing over and covering the trellis with fragrance and color. She picks one, rubbing the soft petals against her face, weathered from time and hard work. She holds the rose to her nose, eyes closed, enjoying its sweet scent.

She continues her walk up the path to the big house where her daughter, son-in-law, and grandchildren live. There are six grandchildren born in boy-girl order, so each boy has a sister to help take care of them. She softly walks in the back door putting her single rose in a vase on the windowsill. Next, she washes her hands and pulls skillets and pans from the cupboards, working quietly.

She hears the children stirring upstairs and knows she only has minutes before they come rumbling down the stairs. This is her favorite part of the day.

The Forgotten Rose

One day, thousands of years ago, as God looked over the earth, He was aware of its beauty. The trees, the grass; it was a picture of perfection. It is true that the earth was a wonderful place, but something seemed to be lacking, so God searched for an answer. He found his answer in me, a tiny little seed. He planted me, and I bloomed into a beautiful rose. There were many other flowers, but I will just tell you about me and my life as a rose.

Adam, the first man on earth, picked me to

place in the long black hair of his beautiful wife, Eve. After eating God's forbidden fruit, Adam tore me from Eve's hair and tossed me away to die, but I shed another seed. The wind blew me to a faraway land where I would spend the cold winter.

The next summer I awoke to the fresh smell of the earth with the ringing laughter of small children. I stayed there for a few weeks unnoticed, but my fragrance was too much for a little boy named Donny. Donny wasn't like other children. He was shy, sensitive and he loved beauty. He examined my every petal in wide-eyed wonder. He carefully lifted me from my home in the soil, and his sticky little hands carried me away. On our journey, another little boy appeared and began to laugh and tease. The unpleasant child was a detestable fellow, with an air of a bully about him. He snatched me from Donny's hands and we went down a country road.

The mean little brat stopped at a chickencoop and found a few lice and other bugs to drop on my petals. Then he took me to a little white house and rang the doorbell. A young girl came to the door and batted her eyelashes at the sight of her visitor. He handed me to her and she immediately lifted me to her nose.

At the same time out came a bug and up her nose it went. She kicked him hard on the knee and dropped me. Once again, I was tossed aside and forgotten but I enjoyed the scene before me. The bully got what he deserved from the deal.

My next ancestor was kicked around for a while from one place to another and I skipped several summers of blooming. A greenhouse operator found me and the next thing I knew I was planted, uprooted, then taken to his greenhouse to be put on display. Not long afterwards, I was fixed into a bouquet with some other roses. An elastic band was put around us to keep us in place. I was very upset because I was used to my freedom.

We were taken into a small hospital room where an old man lay very still. His face was an ashen color and I learned he had cancer of the bone. Surgeons had scraped his bones in hopes of prolonging his life, but progress was slow. The old man never enjoyed my beauty or fragrance because he died the very same day I arrived. My petals drooped as I watched the sadness and sorrow around me. I welcomed the time for wilting and becoming another seed. I felt a need for freshness descending.

For several years I was kept in a big jar with lots of other seeds. My life pattern was at a standstill. One afternoon a careless teenager with his first gun shot a stray bullet, shattering the jar. I traveled around quite a while and ended up in a private Catholic school where I was once again planted. The rich earth of this place and God nourished me into a much more handsome rose than ever before. My petals were like silk, and my fragrance the most splendid in the garden.

Schooling of the girls to become nuns was completed and graduation was near.

Some very gentle Sisters snipped my stem with scissors and put me in a small vase all by myself. The vase was placed in the very front on the altar where I got a good view of the happenings. Each young woman approaching paused in front of me before ascending to the altar to take her final oath. I felt very special that day and the ceremony is one I will never forget. My faith was restored in many ways that day, which was a turning point in my life. I was truly satisfied after that and I felt an abundance of love I had never experienced before.

My next life was a happy one as I was a member of a bride's bouquet. The sunlight shimmered through the stained-glass windows in the church as the bride walked down the aisle. She had a radiant look of happiness upon her face and everything seemed to glow and sparkle. The affair was grand indeed and I made one young lady very happy when she caught me as I was tossed into the air by the bride. The wedding was such a picture of perfection and an event that would be long remembered.

My next seed wasn't planted so I pushed my own way into the earth beside a little schoolhouse. I was much shorter this year, but I was still a very beautiful rose. I would much rather be a small rose that was striking than to be a gangling awkward one. One day a teenage girl quietly came over to me and lifted me from the ground. She carried me in the little school building, down the hall to a room. When we entered it, I could tell it was a biology lab because someone had been dissecting a worm. The room was empty except for a teacher whose head was down on a desk. I could plainly see the reason for her sadness. There on the blackboard was a horrid picture drawn that was clearly intended to upset her. The teacher raised her head and gave a trembling sigh as she noticed the girl holding me out to her.

"I will trade this rose for your smile", the teen said as handed me over. "I'm sorry." All was forgiven as the two began to talk happily. I was placed in a vase as a remembrance for the next few days, then rudely dumped out by a thoughtless janitor who had knocked the vase over while cleaning.

A few years later, I had an unusual escapade. My seed blew to the outskirts of town where I grew once again. This time I was grabbed up by a clown from a nearby circus who stuck me on a cap and bound my stem with a bright colored ribbon. The hat belonged to a dancing kangaroo who also wore a vibrant vest and odd-looking shoes. Lively music played as the kangaroo danced around to the tune. This left me wilted with most of my petals falling off as he performed. The kangaroo received all the applause as I went unnoticed, ending up on the floor to finish dying.

My next blooming took place in a field in Viet Nam. It was in a beautiful field not around any combat. One day a troop of soldiers were marching past and a young soldier picked me for good luck. He was scheduled to go home after Christmas. He put me in his knapsack with his other provisions. That night the men marched through a swamp and into military action. They fought long and hard. The young soldier was killed. In an act of heroic bravery, he lost his own life but saved his squad and commanding officer. I was sad but did not mourn the way he died so proudly serving his country.

Traveling around after that I spent a couple of seasons just watching the world and things going on around me. Boy, did I ever pick a place to grow one year. I sprouted up at Cape Kennedy among the noise of the rockets. The noise seemed to intensify every day, so I did not thrive. Loud noise and overwhelming fumes eventually finished me off. What a way to go!

My next life had a common quality to it. A boy and girl were walking down a country road where I happened to be growing at the time. They were on their way to a teen center where a dance was being held. The boy was really trying to impress her, so he picked me and handed me to his date. Music created a romantic mood as they entered the dance and he held her close to move in for a kiss. She was not impressed by his boldness and in fact she seemed bored. After leaving her date with a sharp slap, she left me laying on the dance floor where I was once again forgotten.

The next time I bloomed I was picked right away by a man in his early twenties. He took me to a run-down neighborhood and stopped at an old building in the poorest section of town. He carried me to an apartment and knocked on the door. A middle-aged woman opened the door. She wore a faded housedress but her big smile was evident. Her son had picked me to give to his dear mother. He had no money but wanted to give her something to show he appreciated the love and devotion she had given him all these years. The whole time I was with the mother she was smiling. When the time came to throw me out after I died, there were tears in her eyes but a smile on her face. She called this her crying smile as she hugged her son.

It is true that I have traveled from place to place with no control of where I would bloom, but my traveling days were growing short and I was getting weary.

My next bloom was again in a greenhouse and once more I was taken to a hospital room. An old woman lay propped up in her bed. She was a small but spry old rascal with peach colored cheeks. Her long gray-white hair was pulled in a bun at the nape of her neck.

Everyone who cared for her in the hospital was fond of her and she kept them going in circles with her lively chatter.

One thing she talked about constantly was seeing her two grandchildren graduate from high school. She had never seen any of her children or grandchildren graduate and this meant the world to her. The two grandchildren looked forward to her presence because they loved her very much. She would make their graduation special and complete. Very unexpectedly the old lady died, and all were heartbroken, especially the grandchildren who would be graduating in just a few days. The grandchildren took me home and nurtured me until the evening of graduation. By special request on the night of the commencement ceremony, I was placed in a vase on the middle of the stage. I represented the presence of the grandmother and I, through her eyes, saw the long-awaited occasion. After all was over and much thought was given to me in honoring their grandmother, my seed was put in a small box which was placed in the grandmother's casket.

My life of roaming is over now. I am at last

content, resting where I belong, once again the forgotten rose.

Mary and Grandma Bright

Mary Whalen

*I am the rose of Sharon,
the lily of the valleys*
Song of Solomon 2:1

Favorite Memories of Grandma

I remember Grandma climbing the cherry tree by her house and picking the cherries. The limb she was on broke and it looked like she floated to the ground. She didn't get hurt and she made cherry cobbler with her pickings. It was so good.

~ Jesse

I always remember grandma working in her garden hoeing and pulling weeds. I went blackberry picking with her once. She always carried a big stick to move the stickers back while we picked. Low and behold, there was a big blacksnake and it scared me almost to death. Grandma took her stick and used it to fling the snake over in the tall weeds never missing a beat, and kept right on picking. She also took me mayapple digging and dried the roots on our old shed's roof. I can still spot those plants in the woods.

~ Mary

I remember Grandma taught me to make kites from newspapers. She always had a ball of cloth and would tear off strips for me so I could use them on the tails of my kites. She made black salve and mustard plasters. I would never cough in front of her after getting one used on me. Grandma was a mountain woman and chewed Union Workman tobacco all her life.

~ Ronnie

Warm summer mornings I would get up early and run down to grandma's house. She made coffee by boiling water with the coffee grounds right in it. Donald and Terri usually were there too. We each had a special cup for our coffee. Mine was yellow and had a chip in the rim. Coffee will stunt your growth is an old saying, but it might be true since we are all short!

~ DeDe

Grandma could make any plant grow. I cut a small pine tree and took it to grandma. She said I shouldn't have cut it down and she would try to fix it. She took a potato and stuck it on the end of the cut tree. Then she planted it close to her house inside an old car tire for protection. Over time, the tree grew really big. The tire had grown into the trunk and years later was still on it about three feet in the air.

~ Donald

I would catch grasshoppers and other bugs in the front yard and put them in a mason jar. Grandma would poke holes in the lid for ventilation. One day I didn't take the time for grandma to punch holes in the lid and caught the bugs and put them in the jar. The next day, grandma found the jar full of dead bugs while I was still in bed at her house. She started making the bed with heavy quilts covering up my head and tucking them tight around me. I woke up scared and started screaming *Grandma, Grandma, let me out I can't breathe.* She said, "Now you know how those little bugs felt in that jar because they didn't have any holes punched in it for air."

~ Terri

About the Author

Mary McKnight-Whalen was born in Columbus, Ohio, in 1948, the second of six children. In 1955, the family moved to rural southeast Ohio where she still resides.

The Forgotten Rose was written to honor her maternal grandmother, Mary Hannah Bright (September 19, 1889 – March 12, 1966).

In 1966, in her senior year in high school, Mary was assigned to write an essay. She chose to write what was close to her heart; her love for her Grandmother and her Grandmother's wish to see her Grandchildren graduate high school.

www.ingramcontent.com/pod-product-compliance
Lightning Source LLC
Chambersburg PA
CBHW052309300426
44110CB00035B/2314